DEDICATION

To my wife Jill, for your constant love, support, and belief in me. You fill my life with laughter, happiness, and hope.

101 QUIRKY & CRAZY PHRASES & SAYINGS

At some time or another we've all said or heard them - those quirky little sayings and phrases that seem to perfectly describe or solve a particular situation.

You know - ones like; "Don't Count Your Chickens Before They Hatch," or "Fast as Greased Lightning." They sound so matter-of-factly and downright smart at the time. But honestly, I never really knew what most of them meant and for sure didn't know where they came from - and most people I know didn't either. So, here's a collection of some I'm sure you're familiar with, complete with their meanings (at least in contemporary terms) and their sometimes very quirky, often bizarre, and perhaps debatable origins. The next time you have the urge to spout one off or a "know-it-all" relative or co-worker does, you'll be ready with some insight for them that will probably leave them speechless!

Enjoy!

CONTENTS

CONTENTS

CONTENTS

"TURN A BLIND EYE"

Meaning

Often used to describe a willful refusal to acknowledge a particular reality or situation.

Origin

Its origins lie with British Naval hero Horatio Nelson. While engaged in the 1801 Battle of Copenhagen, Nelson's ships were pitted against a large Danish-Norwegian fleet. When his superior officer flagged for him to withdraw, the one-eyed Nelson brought his telescope to his bad eye and proclaimed, "I really do not see the signal." He then went on to score a decisive victory!

"SLEEP TIGHT"

Meaning

Wishing someone a good night's sleep.

Origin

During Shakespeare's time, mattresses were secured on bed frames by ropes. In order to make the bed firmer, one had to pull the ropes to tighten the mattress.

"THREE SHEETS TO THE WIND"

Meaning

Having too much alcohol to drink, being drunk.

Origin

Sailors had a lot of terms for being drunk. Being tipsy was 'a sheet in the wind's eye,' and being hammered was a full, 'three sheets to the wind.'

The sheets in question were actually the ropes that held down the sails, so if all three ropes were loose, the sails would billow about like a drunken sailor.

"THE KISS OF DEATH"

Meaning

The Kiss of Death usually marks the end or demise of something.

Origin

This one is rooted in the Italian mafia, where someone who's been marked for death receives the metaphorical 'kiss' prior to their execution.

"BITE THE BULLET"

Meaning

Making the decision to do something that is difficult or unpleasant.

Origin

During wartime, before the days of effective anesthesia, battlefield surgeons had their patients bite down on a bullet in an attempt to distract them from the pain and to protect from biting their own tongues.

"CAUGHT RED-HANDED"

Meaning

To be caught doing something wrong.

Origin

This saying originated because of a law. If someone butchered an animal that didn't belong to them they had to be caught with the animal's blood on their hands to be convicted. Just being caught with freshly cut meat did not make the person guilty.

"BUTTER SOMEONE UP"

Meaning

To flatter someone.

Origin

One belief is that this comes from an ancient Indian custom that involved throwing balls of clarified butter at statues of the gods to seek favor.

Another is that the act of spreading smooth butter on a slice of bread is like spreading nice words on someone.

"EAT HUMBLE PIE"

Meaning

Making an apology and suffering the humiliation along with it.

Origin

During the Middle Ages, the lord of the manor would hold a feast after hunting. He would receive the finest cut of meat at the feast, but those of a lower standing were served a pie filled with the entrails and innards, known as 'umbles.'

Therefore, receiving 'umble pie' was considered humiliating because it informed others in attendance of the guest's lower status.

"KICK THE BUCKET"

Meaning

To die.

Origin

When a cow was killed at the slaughterhouse, a bucket was placed under it while it was positioned on a pulley. Sometimes the animal's legs would kick during the adjustment of the rope and it would literally kick the bucket before being killed.

"SAVED BY THE BELL"

Meaning

To be rescued from an unwanted situation.

Origin

As scary as it sounds, being buried alive was once a common occurrence. People who feared succumbing to such fate were buried in special coffins that connected to a bell above ground. At night, guards listened for any bells in case they had to dig up a living person and save them 'by the bell.'

"MIND YOUR P'S AND Q'S"

Meaning

To mind your manners.

Origin

In the 17th century, English pubs served beer in pints and quarts. Bartenders would keep watch on the alcohol consumption of their patrons and if one was getting unruly, the bartender might warn them to mind their 'p's and q's.'

"BREAK A LEG"

Meaning

Wishing someone good luck.

Origin

The term 'break a leg' originates in the theater. Since superstitions once ran rampant in the theater it's not surprising to learn that wishing someone good luck outright is actually considered bad luck. Instead, it was more suitable to wish ill on someone before a performance, since the opposite was supposed to occur.

"LET THE CAT OUT OF THE BAG"

Meaning

To reveal a secret.

Origin

The phrase, 'letting the cat out of the bag' finds its roots in 18th century street fraud. Suckling pigs were often sold in bags, and a popular scheme was to replace the pig with a cat and sell it to an unwitting victim.

"DON'T LOOK A GIFT HORSE IN THE MOUTH"

Meaning

It's considered rude to inquire about the worth of a present you've received.

Origin

Horses' gums recede with age, leading to longer teeth. A common way to inspect a horse's 'worth' is to check its mouth.

Years ago, receiving a horse as a gift and immediately inspecting its mouth and teeth for value was considered offensive, much like inquiring about the worth of a present today is considered rude.

"CLOSE BUT NO CIGAR"

Meaning

Coming very close to a goal but coming up short.

Origin

Carnivals used to give out cigars as prizes, so almost winning would get you close to achieving a cigar, but not quite.

"SHOW YOUR TRUE COLORS"

Meaning

To reveal one's true nature.

Origin

Warships used to fly multiple flags to confuse their enemies. However, the rules of warfare stated that a ship had to hoist its true flag before firing and hence, display its country's true colors.

"LET YOUR HAIR DOWN"

Meaning

To relax or be at ease.

Origin

Parisian nobles risked condemnation from their peers if they appeared in public without an elaborate hairdo. Some of the more intricate styles required hours of work, so of course it was a relaxing ritual for these aristocrats to come home at the end of a long day and let their hair down.

"BLOOD IS THICKER THAN WATER"

Meaning

Family comes before everything else.

Origin

In ancient Middle Eastern culture, blood rituals between men symbolized bonds that were far greater than even those of family.

The saying also has to do with 'blood brothers,' because warriors who symbolically shared the blood they shed in battle together were said to have stronger bonds than even biological brothers.

"BREAK THE ICE"

Meaning

To commence a project or initiate a friendship.

Origin

Before the days of trains or cars, port cities that thrived on trade suffered during the winter because frozen rivers prevented commercial ships from entering the city. Small ships known as 'icebreakers' would rescue the icebound ships by breaking the ice and creating a path for them to follow.

Before any type of business arrangement today, it is now customary to 'break the ice' before beginning the project.

"YOU'RE PULLING MY LEG"

Meaning

To tease someone or jokingly lie to them.

Origin

This saying comes from the criminal world of the 18th century. Street thieves would literally pull victims down by their leg in order to more easily rob them.

"DON'T THROW THE BABY OUT WITH THE BATHWATER"

Meaning

Hang on to valuable things when getting rid of unnecessary things.

Origin

During the 1500s most people bathed once a year. Even when they did bathe, the entire family used the same tubful of water. The man of the house bathed first, followed by other males, then females, and finally the babies. You can imagine how thick and cloudy the water became by that time, so the infant's mothers had to take care not to throw them out with the bathwater when they emptied the tub.

"MORE THAN YOU CAN SHAKE A STICK AT"

Meaning

Having more of something than you need.

Origin

Farmers controlled their sheep by shaking their staffs to indicate where the animals should go. When farmers had more sheep than they could control, it was said they had 'more than you can shake a stick at.'

"RULE OF THUMB"

Meaning

A common, ubiquitous benchmark.

Origin

Legend has it that 17th century English Judge Sir Francis Buller ruled it was permissible for a husband to beat his wife with a stick, given that the stick was no wider than his thumb.

"SPILL THE BEANS"

Meaning

To reveal a secret.

Origin

In ancient Greece, beans were used to vote for candidates entering various organizations. One container for each candidate was set out before the group members who would place a white bean in the container if they approved of the candidate and a black bean if they did not. Sometimes a clumsy voter would accidentally knock over the jar, revealing all of the beans and allowing everyone to see the otherwise confidential votes.

"JAYWALKER"

Meaning

Someone who crosses the street in a reckless or illegal manner.

Origin

Jay birds that travelled outside of the forest into urban areas often became confused and unaware of the potential dangers in the city traffic. Amused by their erratic behavior, people began using the term 'Jaywalker' to describe someone who crossed the street irresponsibly.

"GO COLD TURKEY"

Meaning

To quit something abruptly.

Origin

People believed that during withdrawal the skin of drug addicts became translucent, hard to the touch, and covered with goosebumps - much like the skin of a plucked turkey.

"CROCODILE TEARS"

Meaning

A display of superficial or false sorrow.

Origin

This myth dates back as far as the 14th century and comes from a book called "The Travels of Sir John Mandeville." Wildly popular upon its release, the tale recounts a brave knight's adventures during his supposed travels through Asia. Upon its many fabrications, the book includes a description of crocodiles that notes, "These serpents slay men, and eat them weeping, and they have no tongue." While factually inaccurate, Mandeville's account of weeping reptiles later found its way into the works of Shakespeare, and 'crocodile tears' became an idiom as early as the 16th century.

"WAKING UP ON THE WRONG SIDE OF THE BED"

Meaning

To wake up in a bad mood.

Origin

For centuries, the left side of the bed or anything having to do with the left was often associated with and considered sinister. To ward off evil, innkeepers made sure the left side of the bed was pushed against the wall so that guests had no other option but to get up on the right side of the bed.

"NO SPRING CHICKEN"

Meaning

Someone who is past their prime.

Origin

New England chicken farmers generally sold chickens in the spring, so the chickens born in the springtime yielded better earnings than the chickens that survived the winter. Sometimes farmers tried to sell old birds for the price of a new spring chicken. Clever buyers complained that the fowl was 'no spring chicken,' and the term came to represent anyone past their prime.

"STAY ON THE STRAIGHT AND NARROW"

Meaning

To generally stay out of trouble.

Origin

This phrase is actually linked to biblical origin. Matthew 7:13/14 described the gates to heaven as "strait" and the way to eternal life as "narrow."

"ONCE IN A BLUE MOON"

Meaning

Something that doesn't happen very often.

Origin

A blue moon is the second full moon in a single calendar month, and is an extremely rare event.

"GIVE THE COLD SHOULDER"

Meaning

A rude way of telling someone they're not welcome.

Origin

Although giving someone the cold shoulder today is considered rude, it was actually regarded as a polite gesture in medieval England. After a feast, the host would let his guests know it was time to leave by giving them a cold piece of meat from the shoulder of beef, mutton, or pork.

"DRESSED TO THE NINES"

Meaning

To dress exceptionally well.

Origin

Although there seems to be no firm consensus on the origin, the most popular theory comes from the fact that the very best suits made used a full nine yards of fabric.

"WHITE ELEPHANT"

Meaning

Any possession that is burdensome.

Origin

White elephants were once considered highly sacred creatures in Thailand, but they were also wielded as a subtle form of punishment. If an underling or rival angered a Siamese king, the royal might present the unfortunate man with the gift of a white elephant. While ostensibly a reward, the creatures were tremendously expensive to feed and house, so caring for one often drove the recipient into financial ruin.

"RUB THE WRONG WAY"

Meaning

To irritate, bother, or annoy someone.

Origin

In colonial America servants were required to wet-rub and dry-rub the oak-board floors each week. Doing it against the grain caused streaks to form, making the wood look awful and irritating the homeowner.

"CAT GOT YOUR TONGUE"

Meaning

Something said when a person is at a loss for words.

Origin

A couple sources for this saying seem to be popular. The first refers to the 'cat-o'-nine-tails' - a whip used by the English Navy for flogging. The whip caused so much pain that the victims were left speechless.

The second refers to the practice of cutting out the tongues of liars and blasphemers and feeding them to cats.

"DIEHARD"

Meaning

Typically refers to someone with a strong dedication to a particular set of beliefs.

Origin

In its earliest incarnation in the 1700s, the expression described condemned men who struggled the longest when they were executed by hanging.

The phrase became even more popular after 1811's Battle of Albuera during the Napoleonic Wars. In the midst of the fight, a wounded British officer named William Inglis supposedly urged his unit forward by bellowing, "Stand your ground and die hard .... and make the enemy pay dearly for each of us!" Inglis' 57th Regiment suffered 75 percent casualties during the battle and went on to earn the nickname 'the Die Hards.'

"RESTING ON YOUR LAURELS"

Meaning

Describing someone who is overly satisfied with their past triumphs.

Origin

The idea of resting on your laurels dates back to the leaders and athletic stars of ancient Greece. In Hellenic times, laurel leaves were closely tied to Apollo, the god of music, prophecy, and poetry. Apollo was usually depicted with a crown of laurel leaves, and the plant eventually became a symbol of stars and achievement. Victorious athletes at the ancient Pythian games received wreaths made of laurel branches, and the Romans later adopted the practice and presented wreaths to generals who won important battles. Venerable Greeks and Romans, or "laureates" were thus able to 'rest on their laurels' by basking in the glory of past achievements. Only since the 1800s did the phrase take on a negative connotation and has been used to describe those who are overly satisfied with past triumphs.

"RUN AMOK"

Meaning

To go Crazy

Origin

This saying comes from the Malaysian word 'amoq' which describes the behavior of tribesmen who, under the influence of opium, became wild, rampaging mobs that attacked anybody in their path.

"PLEASED AS PUNCH"

Meaning

To be very happy.

Origin

A 17th century puppet-show for children called Punch and Judy featured a puppet named Punch who always killed people. The act of killing brought him pleasure, so he felt pleased with himself afterwards.

"GO THE WHOLE NINE YARDS"

Meaning

To try one's best.

Origin

World War II Fighter pilots received a nine-yard chain of ammunition. Therefore, when a pilot used all of his ammunition on one target he gave it, 'the whole nine yards.'

"BY AND LARGE"

Meaning

For the most part or all things considered.

Origin

Many everyday phrases are nautical in origin. As far back as the 16th century, the word 'large' was used to mean that a ship was sailing with the wind at its back.

Meanwhile, the much less desirable 'by' meant the vessel was traveling into the wind.

So, for mariners, 'by and large' referred to trawling the seas in any and all directions relative to the wind.

"THE THIRD DEGREE"

Meaning

When someone undergoes a long or arduous interrogation.

Origin

There are several theories to the origins of this saying but the most likely is derived from the Freemasons, a centuries-old fraternal organization whose members undergo rigorous questioning and examinations before becoming 'third degree' members, or 'master masons.'

"READ THE RIOT ACT"

Meaning

To chastise loudly, or to issue a severe warning.

Origin

In 18th-century England, the Riot Act was a real document and it was often recited aloud to angry mobs. Instituted in 1715, the Riot Act gave the British government authority to label any group of more than 12 people a threat to the peace. In these circumstances, a public official would read the Riot Act and order the people to 'disperse themselves and peaceably leave.' Anyone that remained after one hour was subject to arrest or removal by force.

"EATING CROW"

Meaning

To admit fault or be proved wrong after taking a strong position.

Origin

The Bible lists crow as unfit for eating, and along with buzzards and rats, it was actually illegal to eat crow in the Middle Ages. As such, it was also humiliating to consume it.

"CAN'T HOLD A CANDLE TO"

Meaning

Describing a person or thing that is distinctly inferior to someone or something else.

Origin

Dating back to the 1600s, a lowly apprentice to a master of a craft might only be fit to hold a candle in order to provide light for the master while he works.

"DON'T COUNT YOUR CHICKENS BEFORE THEY HATCH"

Meaning

You shouldn't make plans that depends on something good happening before you know that it has actually happened.

Origin

Dating back to at least the 16th century. It is said to be written in New Sonnets and Pretty Pamphlets by Thomas Howell, in 1570:

"Count not thy chickens that unhatched be,
Waye words as winde, till thou find certainty."

"PAR FOR THE COURSE"

Meaning

What you would expect to happen; something normal or common.

Origin

Believed to have originated from the sport of golfing. In golf, the term 'par' is a common one. Each individual hole, and in some cases the entire course, has a set maximum number of strokes an experienced golfer is expected to take in order to finish it.

"RED TAPE"

Meaning

Anything that may delay or hold us up, whatever the process may be. A lot of unnecessary bureaucracy.

Origin

Dating back to the 16th century, legal and official documents were tied up or bound with red tape and as such were difficult to access and therefore insured that they weren't easily tampered with.

"THAT'S GOING TO COST AN ARM AND A LEG"

Meaning

A common phrase that means it's going to cost to the point of sacrifice. It's going to hurt. The price is high.

Origin

Years ago, before cameras, when portraits were painted, artists charged by the number of limbs that were painted in the portrait. Often the persons arms and hands were behind their back or hidden by their clothing if they wanted a cheaper painting, costing them 'an arm and a leg' if visible, as these were more difficult to paint.

"BIG WIG"

Meaning

Generally thought to be a person of high repute, a wheeler and dealer, someone prominent.

Origin

Back in the early days men and women only bathed occasionally (as bad as that sounds). Men would shave their heads and wear wigs. They couldn't wash their wigs however, so they would hollow out a loaf of bread, place the wig inside, and bake it. This would kill any lice or bugs in the wig, and the wig came out big and fluffy due to the moisture and heat inside the loaf of bread.

"HEARD IT THROUGH THE GRAPEVINE"

Meaning

Something that is heard, unofficially or indirectly.

Origin

Originating at the turn of the century when the telegraph system was being built, it required thousands of miles of wire to be installed. This wire was held in place several feet above the ground with poles at equal intervals. People thought the wires and poles looked like the strings used to train grapevines so the telegraph lines became known as 'the grapevine.' People started referring to hearing things "through the grapevine."

"THE REAL McCOY"

Meaning

This phrase is used in much of the English-speaking world to mean, 'the real thing' or, 'the genuine article.'

Origin

Although attributed to several different origins, two of the most common are;

Originated in Scotland in the 1880s, 'The Real Mackay,' applied to whisky, men and things of the highest quality.

A Canadian inventor, Elijah McCoy, born in 1844, had many different inventions, his first being a revolutionary lubricator for steam engines.

People who have always wanted quality, ask for, "The Real McCoy."

"A SKELETON IN THE CLOSET"

Meaning

A dark or embarrassing secret in someone's past they'd prefer remains undisclosed.

Origin

Prior to the Anatomy Act of 1832 in Britain, doctors weren't allowed to dissect dead bodies for research or teaching students and so had to do so illegally.

After the bodies had been dissected the doctors had to hide the skeletons as they were evidence of a crime and were often hidden in the closet.

"HEADS WILL ROLL"

Meaning

Someone is going to be severely punished for something they did or didn't do.

Origin

This phrase is most commonly associated with the form of capital punishment; beheading, either by Guillotine or Axman.

After being decapitated, the head of the person being executed would often roll around a little before falling into the basket below the blade.

"YOU REAP WHAT YOU SOW"

Meaning

A person's actions dictate the consequences that they will ultimately face.

Origin

This comes from the Bible;

Galatians VI King James Version: Whatsoever a man soweth, that shall he also reap.

"HIGH ON THE HOG"

Meaning

To be or live luxuriously.

Origin

The best cuts of meat on a pig come from the back and upper leg. The wealthy ate cuts from 'high on the hog' while the paupers ate belly pork and trotters.

"DON'T PUT ALL YOUR EGGS IN ONE BASKET"

Meaning

To rely too much on one resource or one line of effort. To risk everything on a single venture.

Origin

Although there is some controversy over the origin of this phrase, it is most commonly attributed to Miguel Cervantes, who wrote Don Quixote in 1605: "Tis the part of wise men to keep himself today for tomorrow, and not venture all his eggs in one basket."

"MAKING A MOUNTAIN OUT OF A MOLEHILL"

Meaning

To escalate a small thing into a big problem.

Origin

The exact origin for this phrase is unknown. However, it is believed to be over 350 years old as it is found in a book of proverbs by James Howell as early as the year 1660.

"ROLL WITH THE PUNCHES"

Meaning

To tolerate or 'roll' with the hardships one may unexpectedly run into.

Origin

Believed to have originated with boxing, where 'rolling with the punches' was a term describing how boxers often angle themselves in certain ways and 'roll' their heads and body to help lessen the impact of incoming blows.

"BEATING A DEAD HORSE"

Meaning

To bring up an issue that has already been resolved.

Origin

This is believed to have originated with horse racing, where horses were often hit or 'beaten' by their jockeys with a riding crop to get them to run faster. The horse responded by either running faster or not at all if it was too tired. There was no longer a point or need in 'beating' the 'dead' horse if it wasn't responding.

"UNDER THE WEATHER"

Meaning

Feeling sick, sad or depressed.

Origin

From nautical origins, when a sailor was feeling seasick he went down below, under the deck, away from the weather to help in his recovery.

"YADA YADA"

Meaning

A way to let a person know that what they're saying is predictable or boring.

Origin

This saying with its current "and so on and so forth" meaning originally appeared somewhere around the mid 1900s. It was popularized by the character Elaine in the television show, 'Seinfeld' in the 1990s.

"THE JIG IS UP"

Meaning

For a ruse or trick to be discovered. To be caught.

Origin

This came from a time when the word jig was slang for 'trick' and dates back to the mid-to-late 16th century where the word became slang for a practical joke or trick.

"IF YOU CAN'T STAND THE HEAT, GET OUT OF THE KITCHEN"

Meaning

If an activity or task is too difficult to do, then perhaps it would be best to stop doing it.

Origin

It's thought that Harry S. Truman coined this phrase, and used it as early as 1942. A newspaper from that year, The Soda Springs Sun, quoted him: "Favorite rejoinder of Harry S. Truman, when a member of his war contacts investigating committee objects to his strenuous pace: 'If you don't like the heat, get out of the kitchen.'"

"NEEDLE IN A HAYSTACK"

Meaning

Something that is very difficult to find.

Origin

One of the earliest uses of this is in the book, 'The Complete Works of Washington Irving' in1834:
"If you want to find any particular article, it is, in the language of an humble but expressive saying, - 'looking for a needle in a haystack.'"

"LONG IN THE TOOTH"

Meaning

Someone or something that is old in age.

Origin

This phrase originates from horses, or more specifically, horse's teeth; as a horse ages their teeth continue to grow making it possible to give an approximation as to how old a horse is simply by looking at their teeth.

"BIRDS OF A FEATHER FLOCK TOGETHER"

Meaning

People tend to associate with those who share similar interests or values.

Origin

This phrase is at least 470 years old, as it goes back to the mid-16th century. William Turner is said to have used a version of this expression in 'The Rescuing of Romish Fox', from the year 1545:

"Byrdes of on kynde and color folk and fly allwayes together."

"BETTER KNOCK ON WOOD"

Meaning

A tongue-in-cheek sort of phrase for when someone has had a lot of good luck, they should be hopeful and careful to avoid the bad luck which may follow.

Origin

From a pagan belief that malevolent spirits inhabited wood, and that if you expressed a hope for the future you should touch or 'knock on wood' to prevent the spirits from hearing and presumably preventing your hopes from coming true.

"FAMOUS LAST WORDS"

Meaning

A remark or prediction that is likely to be proved wrong by events.

Origin

Before its current meaning, years ago it was used to refer to the actual dying words of prominent people and thought to have extreme importance and insight.

"TAKE IT WITH A GRAIN OF SALT"

Meaning

To accept a statement but to maintain a degree of skepticism about its truth.

Origin

This comes from the fact that food is more easily swallowed if taken with a small amount of salt.

This phrase is an ancient one, dating back to Greece in 77A.D. Pliny the Elder translated an antidote for poison which needed the 'grain of salt' added in order to be effective.

"KEEP YOUR NOSE TO THE GRINDSTONE"

Meaning

To apply yourself conscientiously to your work.

Origin

Coming from the practice of knife grinders, who, when sharpening blades would bend over the stone, or even lie down flat with their faces near the grindstone in order to hold the blade close to the stone.

"A PICTURE IS WORTH A THOUSAND WORDS"

Meaning

A picture can often tell a story just as well, if not better than, a lot of written words.

Origin

This phrase emerged in the United States in the early part of the 20th century and is believed to have been used to describe the effectiveness of pictures used in advertising.

"ON A WING AND A PRAYER"

Meaning

In a difficult situation, relying on meager resources and luck to get out of it.

Origin

This phrase originated during WWII and refers to a pilot of a damaged warplane trying to get back to base safely.

It was used in the Hollywood film, 'Flying Tigers', starring John Wayne and also in a hit song by Harold Adamson and Jimmie McHugh.

"THAT'S ALL SHE WROTE"

Meaning

A sudden and unforeseen end to one's hopes or plans.

Origin

The origin of this expression is believed to be the punch line of a sad tale about an American GI serving overseas in WWII. The serviceman is supposed to have received a 'Dear John' letter from his sweetheart. He reads it to his fellow soldiers: "Dear John". 'Well, go on, they say.' "That's it, he says; that's all she wrote."

"FACE THE MUSIC"

Meaning

To accept the unpleasant consequences of one's actions.

Origin

Although its origins are unclear, a couple of accepted versions are;

The tradition of disgraced officers being 'drummed out' of their regiment.

Another popular theory is that it was the actors who 'faced the music'. That is, faced the orchestra pit, when they went on stage.

"UP SHIT CREEK WITHOUT A PADDLE"

Meaning

Being in an awkward situation or unpleasant predicament.

Origin

This slang phrase dates back to the 1860s during the American Civil War. Not an actual place, it was a figurative way of describing somewhere unpleasant; somewhere someone wouldn't want to be. The 'without a paddle' ending was added as an additional intensifier.

"LIKE TWO PEAS IN A POD"

Meaning

Two identical items or people who act, think, or behave alike.

Origin

This dates back to 16th century England and refers to the fact that two peas from the same pod are virtually identical to one another.

"A WOLF IN SHEEP'S CLOTHING"

Meaning

Someone who hides malicious intent under the disguise of kindness.

Origin

This phrase was both used in Aesop's Fables and also in the book of Matthew 7:15 of the King James Version of the Bible.

"AS COOL AS A CUCUMBER"

Meaning

To be calm and relaxed in the face of an uncomfortable or dangerous situation.

Origin

Cucumbers are cool to the touch and this phrase was first recorded in John Gay's Poems, New Song on New similes, 1732:
"I...cool as a cucumber could see the rest of womankind."

"BACK-SEAT DRIVER"

Meaning

Someone who criticizes or advises in a critical manner from the sidelines.

Origin

Dating back to the early part of the 20th century in the USA, automobiles were becoming popular and many people, passengers in the vehicle, started the annoying habit of giving unwanted advice on how to drive to the vehicle driver.

"BURY THE HATCHET"

Meaning

To settle your differences with an adversary.

Origin

This phrase originated with the American Indians. It was a tradition for chiefs of tribes to bury a hatchet when they came together for a peace agreement.

“WHAT YOU SEE IS WHAT YOU GET - WYSIWYG”

Meaning

Referring to or implying that what you see is just that - exactly what you’ll get.

Origin

‘Wysiwyg’ pronounced ‘whizzywig’ is a very popular acronym. Although popular in the computer world today, referring to a computer screen display which appears on screen as it will appear when printed on paper, it’s first thought to have been used by comedian Flip Wilson in performances as his drag character, Geraldine, in ‘Rowan & Martin’s Laugh-In’ television show in the 1960s.

"WHIPPER SNAPPER"

Meaning

Referring to an insignificant person, especially a rude and ill-mannered youngster.

Origin

Dating back to the 1600s, this refers to when many young street kids had a habit of hanging around town, snapping whips to pass the time.

"WIN ONE FOR THE GIPPER"

Meaning

This quotation was used by Ronald Reagan, meaning that when things are going rough, pull together and give it your all.

Origin

This originated in American football. Knute Rockne was the coach of the US Notre Dame team in the1920s and George Gipp was his star player. The story goes that Gipp fell ill and when dying asked Rockne to promise that, when things were going badly for the team, he should inspire them by asking them to 'win one for the Gipper.'

Ronald Reagan played the part of Gipp in the 1940 film, 'Knute Rockne: All American.'

"YELLOW-BELLY"

Meaning

A cowardly person.

Origin

This came from 18th century England as a derogatory nick-name for people born in the Fens of Lincolnshire, supposedly whom had a yellow, sickly complexion from residing in this marshy area.

"YOU CAN LEAD A HORSE TO WATER BUT YOU CAN'T MAKE IT DRINK"

Meaning

People, like horses, will only do what they have a mind to do.

Origin

This saying was recorded as early as 1175 in Old English Homilies.

"AULD LANG SYNE"

Meaning

Old long-since or old long-ago.

Origin

This phrase has been commonplace for Scots and English for centuries, but the best-known use is Robert Burns' poem Auld lang syne, the words of which are sung in English-speaking countries around the world each New Year's Eve, to a tune that Burns said he transcribed from an old man's singing of it.

"DEAD AS A DOORNAIL"

Meaning

Dead, devoid of life (when applied to people, plants or animals).

Finished with, unusable (when applied to inanimate objects).

Origin

This is very old - at least the 14th century. Doornails were large-headed studs that were used for strength in doors. The practice was to hammer the nail through and then bend the protruding end over to secure it. The nail would be unusable afterwards and so considered 'dead.'

"FAST AS GREASED LIGHTNING"

Meaning

To describe or exaggerate something or someone that is very fast.

Origin

The speed of lightning has been known by people for centuries and used for comparison to anything 'fast' when describing such.

Then, during the early 19th century, people added 'greased' to the phrase in order to emphasize and intensify the meaning.

"BAD HAIR DAY"

Meaning

A day when a person's hair seems unmanageable. It also means a day when everything seems to be going wrong.

Origin

This first came into prominence following its use in the 1992 film, 'Buffy the Vampire Slayer'.

Buffy (Kristy Swanson) to the one-armed vampire Amilyn (Paul Reubens):

"I'm fine but you're obviously having a bad hair day."

"DOESN'T KNOW SHIT FROM SHINOLA"

Meaning

Possessing poor judgment or knowledge.

Origin

'Shinola' was a brand of shoe polish manufactured in the USA. The fact that the two commodities in this phrase could possibly be confused is the basis for the phrase. The distinction is well made; only one of them would be good to apply to your shoes and only particularly dim people could be expected to mix them up.

This phrase is typical of the barracks room talk of WWII GIs where it originated.

"FIGHT FIRE WITH FIRE"

Meaning

To respond to an attack or challenge by using a similar method as one's attacker.

Origin

The origin of this phrase was actual fire-fighting techniques that were used by US settlers in the 19th century. They attempted to guard against grass or forest fires by deliberately starting small controllable fires, which they called 'back-fires', to remove any flammable material in advance of a larger fire and so deprive it of fuel.

"GO OVER LIKE A LEAD BALLOON"

Meaning

For something to fail completely and be considered a flop.

Origin

The phrase originated in America in a 'Mom-N-Pop' cartoon that was syndicated in several US newspapers in June 1924.

Perhaps its most celebrated use is the part played in the naming of the English rock band, Led Zeppelin. When discussing the idea of forming a group, The Who's Keith Moon joked, "It would probably go over like a lead balloon" to which John Entwistle replied, "a lead zeppelin!"
Their first album cover featured a black & white photo of the German airship Hindenburg as it was on fire and crashing in 1937.

"BRING HOME THE BACON"

Meaning

To earn money, particularly for one's family. To be financially successful.

Origin

The origin of this phrase is believed to be the story of the Dunmow Flitch. A local couple who, in 1104, impressed the Prior of Little Dunmow with their marital devotion to the point where he awarded them a flitch (a side) of bacon.

The continuing ritual of couples showing their devotion to one another and winning the prize continues in Great Dunmow, Essex every four years to this day.

"ELVIS HAS LEFT THE BUILDING"

Meaning

The show is over-go home.

Origin

"Elvis has left the building" used to be announced at Elvis Presley's concerts to encourage fans to accept that there would be no further encores and to go home.

First used by promoter Horace Logan in 1956 at an Elvis concert at the Shreveport Auditorium in Louisiana.

"THE HEEBIE-JEEBIES"

Meaning

A feeling of anxiety, apprehension, or uneasiness.

Origin

This nonsense rhyming pair came about in the early 1900s in America when William Morgan "Billy" de Beck included it in his cartoon in the October 26th edition of the New York American:

"You dumb ox - why don't you get that stupid look off of your pan - you gimme the heeby jebbys!"

The phrase, 'Heebie jeebies' caught on quickly and soon began appearing regularly in newspapers and books in the US and abroad.

"RUBBING SALT IN THE WOUND"

Meaning

To make a person's shame or pain in an emotional sense, even worse than it is.

Origin

Nautical in origin, once a sailor had been punished by flogging, his comrades would rub salt into his wounds, making them much more painful, but healing the injuries much faster than if they had been left unattended.

"DOG DAY AFTERNOON"

Meaning

A very hot day, making one feel lazy.

Origin

This goes back to the Romans and the days they called the Canicularis Dies, between July 3 and August 11, when the dog star Sirius rises at the same time as the sun. They believed these were the hottest days of the year due to the combined heat of Sirius and the sun at the same time.

"KILLING TWO BIRDS WITH ONE STONE"

Meaning

To succeed in achieving two goals by means of one action or effort.

Origin

From the Greek mythology tale of Daedalus and Icarus, who escaped from the Labyrinth on Crete by flying out after making wings from the feathers of two birds that Daedalus killed by hurtling one stone and killing them both.

"NOT UNTIL THE COWS COME HOME"

Meaning

Not for a long time

Origin

Believed to refer to the unhurried pace of cows as they make their way back to the barn for milking, one of the earliest examples in print is from the comedy, 'The Scornful Lady' in 1616 and includes this line; 'Kiss till the cow come home, kiss close, kiss close knaves'.

ABOUT THE AUTHOR

Michael Schlueter is an author and photographer living with his wife Jill and their two pup dogs on a small farm in Missouri. He enjoys spending time in the great outdoors, seeing new places, and sharing laughs with family and friends.

Made in the USA
San Bernardino, CA
25 November 2019